The Urgency Of The Multi-Model Approach In Learning Environmental Physics To Achieve Learning Goals

Nurasyah Dewi Napitupulu

Department of Physics Education
Faculty of Teacher Training and Education
Tadulako University, Indonesia

ACKNOWLEDGEMENTS

I would like to express my heartfelt gratitude to all those who have contributed to the completion of this book, "The Urgency of the Multi-Model Approach in Learning Environmental Physics to Achieve Learning Goals."

First and foremost, I would like to extend my sincere appreciation to the Department of Physics Education at the Faculty of Teacher Training and Education, Tadulako University, Indonesia, for providing the necessary support and resources throughout the research and writing process.

I am deeply grateful to my esteemed colleagues and fellow researchers in the field of Environmental Physics education who have shared their knowledge, insights, and experiences, enriching the content of this book. Their valuable contributions have greatly enhanced the quality and depth of the discussions presented.

I would like to extend my heartfelt thanks to the students of the Physics Education program at Tadulako University, whose participation in the research has been instrumental in shaping the ideas and perspectives presented in this book. Their enthusiasm, dedication, and willingness to engage in the learning process have been truly inspiring.

I would also like to acknowledge the assistance and guidance provided by my mentors and advisors throughout this journey. Their expertise, encouragement, and invaluable feedback have been instrumental in shaping the content and structure of this book.

I am also appreciative of the academic institutions and organizations that have helped and supported my research efforts by giving me access to pertinent material, research resources, and chances for professional growth.

Last but not least, I would like to express my deepest appreciation to my family and friends for their unwavering support, encouragement, and understanding throughout the process of writing this book. Their constant love, patience, and belief in me have been a constant source of motivation and inspiration.

This book would not have been possible without the combined efforts, direction, and assistance of everyone indicated above. I am really appreciative of their efforts and am hoping that this book will be a useful tool for students, scholars, and teachers.

Nurasyah Dewi Napitupulu

Department of Physics Education
Faculty of Teacher Training and Education
Tadulako University, Indonesia

CONTENTS

ABSTRACT

Some learning models that can improve creative thinking skills are CPS (Creative Problem Solving), IBL (Inquiry-Based Learning), JUCAMA (Problem Submission and Solving), PBL (Problem Based Learning), SSCS (Search, Solve, Create, Share), Quantum Learning, PjBL (Project Based Learning) and PQ4R (Preview, Question, Read, Reflect, Recite, Review).

However, the combination of IBL, PBL, and PjBL models in one teaching activity is essential to create exciting and dynamic learning conditions. These three models have a more structured learning syntax than the other models. The IBL learning model has advantages in cognitive aspects, helping students develop advanced cognitive abilities such as creative thinking, problem-solving, and communication skills.

The PBL model has advantages in the effective part, namely, making students active in learning. The PBL learning model has advantages in the psychomotor aspect, namely being able to assist students in improving the skills of the questioning process and communicating their knowledge. By applying these three models in learning, it is hoped that a model can be realized to improve students' creative thinking skills more optimally in order to achieve learning goals.

The abstract explains several learning models that can enhance creative thinking skills. These learning models include :

1. CPS (Creative Problem Solving)
   A learning model that encourages students to develop creative thinking in problem-solving.

2. IBL (Inquiry-Based Learning)

   A research-based learning model that helps students develop advanced cognitive abilities such as creative thinking, problem-solving, and communication skills.

3. JUCAMA (Problem Submission and Solving)

   A learning model that involves students in proposing and solving problems.

4. PBL (Problem Based Learning)

   A learning model that focuses on problem-solving, actively involving students in the learning process.

5. SSCS (Search, Solve, Create, Share)

   A learning model that encompasses steps of information search, problem-solving, creativity, and knowledge sharing.

6. Quantum Learning

   A learning model that integrates physical, emotional, social, and intellectual aspects to create a dynamic learning environment.

7. PjBL (Project Based Learning)

   A project-based learning model that engages students in real-world projects to develop creative thinking skills.

8. PQ4R (Preview, Question, Read, Reflect, Recite, Review)

   A learning model involving steps such as previewing before reading, questioning, reading, reflecting, reciting, and reviewing the material.

The abstract also emphasizes the significance of combining the IBL, PBL, and PjBL models in a teaching activity to create exciting and dynamic learning conditions. These three models have a more structured learning syntax compared to other models.

IBL has advantages in cognitive aspects, helping students develop advanced cognitive abilities such as creative thinking, problem-solving, and communication skills. The PBL model excels in the affective domain, making students actively engaged in learning. Additionally, the PBL model benefits the psychomotor aspect by assisting students in improving their questioning skills and communicating their knowledge.

By implementing these three models in education, it is hoped that an optimal model can be realized to enhance students' creative thinking skills and achieve learning goals.

I. INTRODUCTION

Learning is a deliberate and purposeful process that involves the design of activities to facilitate learning within individuals. It is a set of intentional events created to support and enhance the learning process. Learning models, on the other hand, are plans or patterns that shape curricula, instructional materials, and teaching methods in various educational settings. These models provide a conceptual framework that organizes the learning process and guides educators in planning effective teaching activities.

In the field of physics education, it is crucial to employ suitable learning models to achieve the desired learning objectives. These objectives encompass the improvement of cognitive, affective, and psychomotor aspects. Different learning models are designed to target specific aspects of learning. Some models focus on a single aspect, while others aim to address two or even all three aspects simultaneously. However, a comprehensive learning model should encompass all three elements simultaneously, emphasizing cognitive, affective, and psychomotor aspects to create a well-rounded learning experience.

A multi-learning model approach is created when many learning models are combined in the educational process. With the coherent integration of many learning models, this strategy actively incorporates students in the learning process. It stimulates students' active engagement, critical thinking, and problem-solving abilities through a multifaceted learning experience. The teaching of physics disciplines may also use this multi-learning model method, creating a thorough and interesting learning environment.

The use of a multi-learning model approach in physics education offers numerous benefits. It promotes student engagement and involvement by integrating different learning strategies and methods. It encourages students to take an active role in their learning, fostering a deeper understanding of physics concepts and principles. By incorporating various learning models, educators can cater to the diverse learning needs and preferences of students, promoting inclusivity and enhancing the overall learning experience.

The multi-learning model method is very beneficial in physics education since it allows students to acquire critical thinking skills, problem-solving ability, and scientific curiosity. It motivates students to study, question, and explore scientific phenomena, therefore improving their comprehension and mastery of physics ideas. Students may apply their knowledge and abilities to real-world problems through hands-on activities, collaborative projects, and inquiry-based learning.

The introduction emphasizes the deliberate and purposeful character of learning, as well as the need of using appropriate learning models to achieve desired learning outcomes in physics education. It highlights the need of addressing cognitive, emotional, and psychomotor components in order to create an all-encompassing learning experience. A multi-learning model method that integrates various learning models offers a viable way for improving physics teaching, promoting student engagement and critical thinking, and facilitating meaningful learning experiences. Educators may develop dynamic and successful learning environments that allow students to become active learners and accomplish their physics learning goals by using this strategy.

1.1 The Literature Review of Learning Environmental

Gómez-Tejedor J A, Vidaurre A, Tort-Ausina I, Molina-Mateo J, Serrano M-A, Meseguer-Dueñas J M, Martínez Sala R M, Quiles S and Riera J Effectiveness of flip teaching on engineering students' performance in the physics lab Computers & Education

This research paper investigates the effectiveness of flip teaching (FT) in improving engineering students' performance in the physics lab. The study compares the academic results of students who followed a traditional teaching method (TM) with those who followed an FT model. The results indicate that students performed better in both subjects under FT compared to TM. The use of ICT, such as recorded videos, was found to be beneficial in the FT model. The study also explores the impact of FT on different levels of students' academic achievement.

Overall, this research paper provides valuable insights into the effectiveness of flip teaching in the context of physics and electricity courses. The study utilizes a large sample size over multiple academic years, enhancing the reliability of the findings. The introduction of the FT model gradually and the reduction of the teacher's role to answering questions demonstrate a well-planned implementation strategy.

Unfortunately, the research doesn't go into great depth on the precise teaching approaches used in the FT model. Understanding the particular aspects of the flipped classroom strategy that contributed to the enhanced academic achievement would have been helpful. Furthermore, the study does not offer a thorough evaluation of how FT affects students' academic progress at various levels. More thorough investigation may have revealed more complex findings.

While the study highlights the positive impact of the flipped classroom model on laboratory grades and academic performance, it does not thoroughly investigate the reasons behind these improvements. Future research could delve deeper into the underlying mechanisms through which the flipped classroom model enhances learning outcomes.

And also, the paper acknowledges the need for further research to explore the applicability of the flipped classroom model in other disciplines. It would have been valuable to discuss potential challenges or limitations in implementing the FT model in different subject areas and explore strategies to overcome them.

In summary, this study adds to the body of knowledge on flip teaching's efficacy in technical degree programs. The results imply that the flipped classroom paradigm, assisted by ICT, can produce better academic results. To fully comprehend the mechanics and possible constraints of the flipped classroom model in various educational situations, more thorough study and more research are required.

Williams CC, Hecker KG, Paget MK, Coderre SP, Burak KW, Wright B and Krigolson OE. The application of reward learning in the real world: Changes in the reward positivity amplitude reflect learning in a medical education context International Journal of Psychophysiology

This study investigated the relationship between the reward positivity component of the human event-related brain potential (ERP) and the learning process. Participants in a medical education context learned to diagnose liver and biliary diseases. The results showed that as participants learned, the amplitude of the reward positivity decreased. This suggests that the reward positivity is involved in learning across various contexts. The study also demonstrated the effectiveness of reinforcement learning in a medical setting.

The overall findings of this study offer important new understandings of the function of reward positivity in learning. The researchers were able to show how their findings may be used in actual learning settings by utilizing a framework for medical education that exists in the real world. The study's findings are given more validity since EEG data were used to gauge the reward positivity component.

There are certain restrictions to take into account, though. First off, the study's exclusive emphasis on liver and biliary disorders may have limited the findings' applicability to other medical specialties. Also, the study did not examine how well the information was retained over time, which would have revealed additional information on the function of reward positivity in memory consolidation.

Also, the study did not look at how individual characteristics, such as prior knowledge or cognitive skills, may have an impact on the observed increases in reward positivity. By using a more varied sample and investigating the long-term impacts of learning on reward positivity, future study may be able to overcome these constraints.

Despite these drawbacks, the work advances our knowledge of the brain mechanisms underpinning learning and emphasizes the reward positivity's potential as a biomarker for learning processes. The results of more study in this field may have an impact on instructional strategies and treatments designed to improve learning outcomes.

Lerum Ø, Eikeland Tjomsland H, Leirhaug PE, McKenna J, Quaramby T, Bartholomew J, Jenssen E S, Smith A-D and Resaland G K. The Conforming, The Innovating and The Connecting Teacher: A qualitative study of why teachers in lower secondary school adopt physically active learning Teaching and Teacher Education

This study examines the reasons why teachers in lower secondary schools adopt physically active learning (PAL). The researchers conducted interviews with 13 teachers in Norwegian schools and analyzed the data thematically. The findings reveal three teacher personas who adopt PAL: The Conforming Teacher, The Innovating Teacher, and The Connecting Teacher. Teachers adopt PAL to enhance teaching and learning, adhere to school policy, be innovative educators, and because it aligns with their personal positive experiences. The study emphasizes the importance of ongoing support from school leaders and the need for comprehensive professional development programs.

Overall, this study provides valuable insights into the motivations behind teachers' adoption of physically active learning in schools. The thematic analysis of the interviews helps to identify different teacher personas and their reasons for implementing PAL. The findings highlight the multifaceted benefits of PAL, including improved concentration, motivation, engagement, and collaboration among students.

Unfortunately, the study has some limitations. Firstly, the sample size of 13 teachers may not be representative of all teachers in lower secondary schools. A larger sample would provide a more comprehensive understanding of the factors influencing PAL adoption. Additionally, the study focuses on Norwegian schools, which may limit the generalizability of the findings to other educational contexts.

The research also does not go into detail on the precise sorts of assistance that might be most useful in boosting PAL adoption, even while it emphasizes the significance of ongoing support from school officials. Future studies can examine the precise methods and tools that make PAL adoption in classrooms easier.

By identifying the reasons for teachers' acceptance of PAL, this study, in its final analysis, adds to the body of knowledge already available on physically active learning. The research can help build teacher preparation programs and offer guidance to legislators and school administrators. To address the study's shortcomings and investigate the precise support systems required for PAL implementation success, more research is necessary.

Guo P, Saab N, Post L S and Admiraal W. A review of project-based learning in higher education: Student outcomes and measures International Journal of Educational Research

The many outcomes assessed in research on project-based learning (PjBL) in higher education are covered in this section. Learning techniques, emotional results, behavioral outcomes, and artifact performance are among the consequences. These outcomes were measured using a variety of tools, including questionnaires, rubrics, exams, interviews, observation sheets, self-reflection diaries, and artifacts. The part stresses how crucial it is to assess the final products produced by students in PjBL. The evaluation of the research revealed that many lacked precise explanations of measuring methods and data processing, nevertheless. There were studies that did not clearly state the questionnaire items that were utilized, and there were studies that did not clearly state the reliability and validity of scales.

The research advised the adoption of standardized audit techniques since the examination of qualitative data was similarly constrained. The research recommends using log data as a technique of data gathering to give a more thorough insight of student learning. Further experimental study is required to assess the impact of PjBL on student learning outcomes, even though some studies have shown that it improves students' topic knowledge, learning techniques, abilities, motivation, and product quality. The research also analyzes the effects of project-based learning in higher education and recommends promoting its use to develop students' capacity for creativity.

The lack of clear descriptions of measurement instruments and data analysis in many of the reviewed studies is a significant limitation. Without this information, it becomes challenging to evaluate the validity and reliability of the findings. Additionally, the limited analysis of qualitative data suggests a need for more rigorous qualitative research methods in studying PjBL. The study's recommendation to use log data as a data collection method is interesting, as it can provide a more comprehensive understanding of student learning.

The research does not, however, offer detailed instructions on how to successfully gather and analyze log data. Also, although mentioning the advantages of PjBL for a number of outcomes, the study does not offer a thorough examination of its overall effects on student learning. To identify the causal connection between PjBL and student learning results, more experimental study is required. Notwithstanding these drawbacks, the study emphasizes the benefits of project-based learning in higher education and promotes its use to help students become more innovative.

II. Research and Method

The research methodology employed in this study involved a field study approach, which incorporated classroom observations, documentation analysis, and interviews. The primary objective was to gather comprehensive data on the implementation of lectures, curriculum content, learning tools, and students' interest in Environmental Physics.

Classroom observations served as a valuable means to obtain firsthand information regarding the actual execution of lectures. By observing the teaching process, researchers were able to gain insights into how the learning models were applied and their effectiveness in promoting creative thinking skills. Additionally, classroom observations allowed researchers to assess the level of student engagement and participation in the learning activities.

Documentation studies were conducted to analyze the curriculum and learning materials used in the Environmental Physics course. This involved a thorough examination of the syllabus, lesson plans, textbooks, and supplementary resources. By analyzing the documentation, researchers could identify the specific learning models incorporated in the curriculum and the extent to which they aligned with the desired learning objectives. This analysis provided valuable insights into the structure and content of the course and its potential impact on students' creative thinking skills.

In order to gather students' perspectives and insights, interviews were conducted. Students were selected based on a diverse range of backgrounds and academic abilities to ensure a comprehensive understanding of their interests in Environmental Physics. The interviews aimed to explore their perceptions of the subject, their level of engagement, and their experiences with the different learning models employed. Through these interviews, researchers could gather qualitative data that shed light on the students' attitudes towards the learning process and the effectiveness of the multi-model approach in enhancing their creative thinking skills.

The data collected through classroom observations, documentation analysis, and interviews were analyzed using qualitative research methods. This involved a systematic and in-depth examination of the collected data to identify patterns, themes, and relationships. The findings from this analysis were then used to support the arguments and conclusions presented in the study.

It is important to note that ethical considerations were taken into account throughout the research process. Informed consent was obtained from the participants, and their confidentiality and privacy were strictly maintained. The research was conducted in accordance with ethical guidelines and regulations to ensure the integrity and reliability of the findings.

Overall, the research technique used in this work enabled a thorough examination of how various learning models were implemented in the context of environmental physics. Researchers were able to gather important insights on the efficiency of the multi-model method in boosting creative thinking abilities and accomplishing the targeted learning goals by combining classroom observations, documentation analysis, and interviews. The results of this study add to the body of knowledge already known in the field of education and offer useful recommendations for teachers looking to improve the physics teaching and learning process.

III. Results and Discussion

The observations of Environmental Physics lectures in two classes revealed that a specific learning model with a clear syntax was not employed. The lectures were conducted in group settings, with 5-6 students presenting their group assignments through PowerPoint presentations. These group assignments were assigned at the beginning of the course by the lecturer. Following the presentations, a question-and-answer session took place, facilitated by the lecturer. However, only a small number of students actively participated in the discussion, typically those seated in the front rows. Video recordings indicated that many students engaged in conversations or did not attend the lectures, and some students even lacked continuous engagement throughout the entire session

The PowerPoint presentations by the students were primarily text-based, lacking visual appeal. Additionally, only one student presented, often demonstrating poor communication skills and a limited grasp of the material. During the question-and-answer segment, it was observed that the presenting students were often the ones responding. These factors likely contributed to the disengagement of numerous students from the lectures. At the end of the course, the lecturer provided a review of the lecture material and summarized the questions and answers.

The implementation of Environmental Physics lectures primarily took place in lecture halls, with the lecturers functioning as the primary source of knowledge. However, the course material encompassed physics concepts related to the environment, such as sound physics pertaining to background noise and environmental pollution. Nevertheless, the learning approach remained focused on theoretical issues, with limited practical applications. Direct education on global ecological problems could only be achieved through field studies. The enhancement of students' abilities occurred through stages that provided flexibility in building knowledge based on their own experiences driven by curiosity. As such, inquiry-based learning (IBL) was introduced as a means to guide students through the exploration of environmental phenomena, specifically climate change (PI).

The results of unstructured interviews conducted with five student groups (consisting of 5-6 students per group) shed light on their reasons for interest or disinterest in Environmental Physics lectures. The findings, as summarized in Table 1, indicated that the majority of students lacked interest in the lecture material. Group 1 expressed interest solely because no other elective courses were available. Similarly, all members of groups 2, 3, and 4 shared a lack of interest. However, in group 5, some students expressed interest while others did not, citing different reasons.

Overall, it can be concluded that most students were not interested in Environmental Physics lectures. Notably, the reasons for interest revolved around curiosity regarding physics concepts related to the environment. Conversely, the reasons for disinterest included feeling compelled to take the course, perceiving it as unrelated to their field of study (biology, chemistry, social sciences, economics), and finding the lectures predominantly theoretical with a focus on paper and presentation tasks rather than practical applications. These findings were consistent with the observations made during the lectures, where many students displayed disengagement due to their lack of interest in the lecture material.

Group	Interest	Reasons
1	Not interested	There are no other elective courses
2	Interested	Want to know physics formulas related to the environment and want to know what physical theories can be applied to the environment
3	Not interested	Because the course material is related to other subjects, such as Biology, Chemistry, Social Society, Economics
4	Not interested	Just learn the theory, and the task is to make papers and presentations. Do you want an action to be useful for others?
5	Mostly not interested	Some are interested in the reason that the lecture material discusses environmental damage, which is a trend worldwide like global warming Some are not interested because they are forced to contract because they have no other choice

Table 1

Student Interest in Environmental Physics Courses

The table provides a breakdown of the interests and reasons expressed by different groups of students regarding their engagement with Environmental Physics courses. Here is a more detailed explanation of each group's response:

- **Group 1: Not interested**

Reason : The students expressed a lack of interest in Environmental Physics courses, and the main reason provided was that there were no other elective courses available. As a result, it can be inferred that their interest in the subject matter was not the driving factor for their enrollment.

- **Group 2: Interested**

Reason : The students in this group displayed an interest in Environmental Physics. They expressed a desire to learn physics formulas related to the environment and understand the application of physical theories to environmental issues. Their interest stemmed from a curiosity about the practical implications of physics in the context of the environment.

- **Group 3: Not interested**

Reason : The students in this group indicated a lack of interest in Environmental Physics courses. They cited the course material as being related to other subjects such as Biology, Chemistry, Social Sciences, and Economics. It suggests that they perceived the content of Environmental Physics as overlapping with these other subjects, leading to a diminished interest.

- **Group 4: Not interested**

Reason : The students in this group expressed a disinterest in Environmental Physics courses. They mentioned that the focus was primarily on theoretical learning, with assignments centered around writing papers and making presentations. Their lack of interest stemmed from a desire for more practical and action-oriented learning experiences rather than solely acquiring theoretical knowledge.

- **Group 5: Mostly not interested**

Reason : The students in this group displayed mixed levels of interest in Environmental Physics courses. Some were interested in the lecture material, particularly its discussion of global environmental damage and trends like global warming. On the other hand, some students expressed a lack of interest due to being compelled to take the course, likely due to limited alternative options. It suggests that their motivation to engage with the subject was varied, with some finding relevance in environmental issues while others felt restricted in their choices.

This fact is supported by the results of lecture observations where most of the students are not involved in class discussions due to their lack of interest in the lecture material. Based on psychological theory, interest essentially gives pleasure, interest, self-awareness, solid drives and motives, and a person's active involvement in a particular field. The results showed that interest in learning affects learning achievement because it can remember learning in the long term.

As a strong drive from within, interest is a form of intrinsic motivation that can be developed. In the context of learning, research results show that inspiration can increase due to the influence of approaches, methods, or learning models. Based on the literature study and field studies, it was found that there was a discrepancy between the planned learning outcomes and the real ones.

Likewise, learning activities are not by the objectives of the lecture. The description of ecological competence through interviews with lecturers of Environmental Physics courses and student interest in Environmental Physics shows weaknesses and deficiencies in Environmental Physics lectures that need to be improved. For this reason, it is necessary to design lessons with a specific syntax with directly relevant lecture materials on environmental issues that can improve student competence as a whole (cognitive, affective, and psychomotor/skills).

The study results revealed that students were not actively involved in lectures, and Environmental Physics lectures were carried out using the method and approach of giving group assignments, discussions, and presentations. In order to obtain information about the competence of talks, interviews were conducted with the Environmental Physics course lecturers. Through this interview, it was revealed that the assessment carried out was only on cognitive competence.

The field study found a description of the problems of environmental phenomena, which are environmental issues globally and locally. Three ecological issues are interrelated with each other and of global concern, namely climate change (PI), deforestation (DeF), and the use of energy sources (PSE). The different characteristics of these three environmental issues require the design of lectures with a specific syntax to teach the environment through physics concepts.

The lecture approach is in the form of assignment of lecture topics as group assignments communicated through presentations in front of the class.

Material enrichment was obtained through group question and answer presentations with other groups. Lecturers become facilitators in completing questions and answers and giving conclusions on the display material. In this condition, the observations show that there are students who are not involved in in-class discussions and do not even pay attention at all. For this reason, it is necessary to design lectures with learning tools and instruments that can stimulate student interest in environmental physics lessons.

3.1 The Importance of Application of Environmental Physics Learning Multimodel

The use of multimodel learning in Environmental Physics education provides a comprehensive and holistic approach to teaching and learning. It integrates various learning models, strategies, and techniques to create a dynamic and engaging learning environment that fosters students' cognitive, affective, and psychomotor development.

One of the key learning models incorporated in multimodel learning is Inquiry-Based Learning (IBL). IBL encourages students to formulate questions, seek solutions, and engage in problem-solving to satisfy their curiosity. It promotes critical thinking, independent inquiry, and the exploration of theories and ideas related to the world. By presenting students with problems or challenges, IBL stimulates their curiosity and motivates them to explore and learn. The teacher plays a vital role in this process by creating interactions and providing guidance to students.

For example, in an Environmental Physics class, students may be presented with a problem related to environmental pollution. They are encouraged to ask questions, conduct research, and analyze data to gain a deeper understanding of the problem. Through this process, they develop critical thinking skills and become active participants in their learning journey.

Problem-Based Learning (PBL) is another essential component of multimodel learning. PBL focuses on real-world problems and challenges students to find solutions through collaborative and investigative efforts. It requires students to apply their knowledge and skills to address environmental issues and develop problem-solving abilities. By working in groups, students can brainstorm ideas, conduct research, and propose innovative solutions.

An energy-efficient system for a town, for instance, would be the assignment for students in an Environmental Physics class. Analyzing energy sources, looking into renewable energy choices, and creating a strategy that takes environmental sustainability into account would all be necessary. During this project, students practice critical thinking, investigation, and knowledge application to address current environmental issues.

Project-Based Learning (PjBL) is also integrated into multimodel learning to provide students with in-depth investigations of specific topics. PjBL allows students to explore a particular subject matter through hands-on projects, fostering a deeper understanding and application of knowledge. Students undertake research, gather information, and synthesize their findings to produce meaningful outcomes.

In a course on environmental physics, for instance, students may work on a project to investigate how noise pollution affects marine life. Data would be gathered, noise pollution impacts would be examined, and mitigation tactics would be suggested. Students are encouraged to think critically, work in groups, and come up with useful solutions to environmental problems thanks to this project-based learning strategy.

Due to the particular character of the subject, the use of multimodel learning in the field of Environmental Physics education is extremely significant. Environmental Physics covers a wide variety of subjects that necessitate a multidisciplinary approach, combining ideas from physics, environmental science, and other disciplines. It is concerned with comprehending the interconnections of the physical world and the environment, such as the influence of human activities on natural systems, climate change, pollution, and sustainable energy solutions.

Traditional learning approaches in Environmental Physics often rely on the transmission of information, where teachers act as the main source of formulas, laws, and theoretical concepts. While this approach can provide students with foundational knowledge, it may limit their engagement and critical thinking skills. Students may passively receive information without actively applying it to real-world problems or developing a deeper understanding of the subject matter.

Multimodel learning, on the other hand, offers a more student-centered and interactive approach to education. It encourages active participation, critical thinking, and problem-solving skills development. By integrating different learning models, such as IBL, PBL, and PjBL, students are actively engaged in the learning process and can develop a deeper understanding of Environmental Physics concepts.

In an Environmental Physics classroom using multimodel learning, students are no longer passive recipients of information but become active participants in their learning. They are encouraged to ask questions, explore various sources of information, conduct experiments, collaborate with peers, and apply their knowledge to real-world scenarios. This approach fosters critical thinking skills, independent inquiry, and problem-solving abilities, which are crucial for addressing complex environmental challenges.

For example, in an IBL activity, students might be presented with a problem related to noise pollution in a specific environment. They would then formulate hypotheses, collect data, and analyze the impact of noise pollution on the ecosystem. Through this process, they not only gain a better understanding of the underlying physics principles but also develop critical thinking skills as they evaluate evidence, propose explanations, and draw conclusions.

Students may be asked to develop an energy-efficient solution for a community as part of a PBL assignment. They would study on various energy sources, evaluate their effects on the environment, and put forth a sustainable energy strategy. Students may use their knowledge, exercise their creativity, and work together to develop novel solutions to pressing environmental problems using this project-based learning methodology.

Multimodel learning empowers students to become active learners, capable of applying their knowledge and skills to solve complex environmental problems. It encourages them to think critically, collaborate with peers, and develop a deep understanding of the interconnectedness between physics and the environment.

By incorporating multimodel learning in Environmental Physics education, students gain not only a solid foundation of knowledge but also the ability to think critically, analyze data, and propose solutions to real-world environmental challenges. They become active agents of change who can contribute to creating a more sustainable and environmentally conscious society.

1. *Inquiry-Based Learning (IBL)*

The combination of three learning models in Environmental Physics learning, as depicted in Table 2, refers to the syntax or sequence of these models. These models play a crucial role in supporting students' creativity and critical thinking patterns when it comes to understanding and solving problems related to environmental physics.

Stage	Syntax
1	Orientation (Teacher gives problems)
2	Formulate the problem
3	Formulating Hypotheses
4	Collecting data
5	Testing Hypotheses
6	Draw a conclusion

Table 2

Syntax of Inquiry-Based Learning (IBL)

Table 2 outlines the stages and syntax of the three learning models in Environmental Physics. Here is a detailed explanation of each stage :

1. Orientation (Teacher gives problems)

In this stage, the teacher presents the problems or challenges related to environmental physics that students will work on. It serves as an introduction to the learning process.

Example: The teacher presents a problem related to environmental pollution caused by industrial waste. Students are introduced to the problem and its significance in the context of environmental physics.

2. Formulate the problem

Students are encouraged to define and articulate the problem clearly. They identify the key aspects and parameters of the problem they need to address.

Example: Students define the problem statement clearly, such as "How does industrial waste affect the quality of water in nearby ecosystems?" They identify the variables involved, such as the type of waste, the water quality parameters, and the specific ecosystems affected.

3. Formulating Hypotheses

In this stage, students generate hypotheses or educated guesses about potential explanations or solutions to the problem at hand. This step fosters critical thinking and encourages students to consider various possibilities.

Example: Students generate hypotheses, such as "Increased levels of industrial waste in water ecosystems lead to a decrease in biodiversity" or "Industrial waste contamination increases the acidity levels of water bodies."

4. Collecting data

Students collect relevant data and information through various means, such as conducting experiments, gathering research, or analyzing existing data. This stage emphasizes the importance of data collection to support the investigation.

Example: Students conduct fieldwork and collect water samples from various locations near industrial sites. They also gather data from published studies, government reports, and relevant scientific literature to supplement their research.

5. Testing Hypotheses

Students design experiments or methods to test their hypotheses. They analyze the collected data and evaluate whether their hypotheses are supported or refuted by the evidence. This step promotes scientific inquiry and the application of critical thinking skills.

Example: Students design experiments or conduct statistical analysis on the collected data to test their hypotheses. They compare water quality parameters, such as pH, oxygen levels, and presence of pollutants, between contaminated and uncontaminated sites.

6. Draw a conclusion

Based on the data analysis, students draw conclusions and make inferences. They interpret the results of their investigations and reflect on the implications for the environmental physics problem they were addressing. This stage encourages students to think critically and make connections between their findings and the broader context of environmental physics.

Example: Based on their data analysis, students draw conclusions such as "The presence of industrial waste in water ecosystems is correlated with a decrease in species diversity" or "Industrial waste contamination leads to increased acidity levels in nearby water bodies." They discuss the implications of their findings on environmental conservation and propose potential solutions to mitigate industrial pollution.

By following the stages and syntax of these learning models, students engage in active learning, critical thinking, and problem-solving. They develop a deeper understanding of environmental physics concepts and gain practical skills to address real-world environmental challenges.

Scientific inquiry learning provides students with opportunities to actively engage in the scientific process and develop important scientific skills. Here are detailed explanations and examples of each approach :

1. Discovery learning

Discovery learning encourages students to construct their own understanding of scientific concepts through hands-on experiences and active exploration. For example, in an Environmental Physics class, students may investigate the effects of different soil types on water filtration by designing and conducting their own experiments. Through this process, they discover the relationship between soil composition and water quality.

2. Interactive demonstration

In interactive demonstrations, the teacher poses questions that stimulate student responses and promote critical thinking. For instance, the teacher might demonstrate the principles of air pollution using a smoke chamber and ask students to explain the observed phenomena. This approach encourages students to actively participate in the learning process and develop a deeper understanding of the topic.

3. Inquiry lesson

Inquiry lessons involve more complex science experiments that go beyond simple demonstrations. Students actively engage in the scientific process by formulating questions, designing experiments, collecting data, and analyzing results. For example, students may investigate the factors influencing the rate of plant growth in different environmental conditions, such as varying light intensity or nutrient availability. This approach promotes critical thinking and problem-solving skills.

4. Inquiry lab

In inquiry labs, students participate in guided discussions and collaborative activities to investigate scientific phenomena and develop scientific reasoning skills. They work in groups to explore specific research questions and analyze data to draw conclusions. For instance, students might investigate the impact of temperature on the behavior of aquatic organisms by conducting experiments and analyzing their findings.

5. Real-world application

Real-world application involves challenging students to apply their knowledge and skills to authentic, real-life contexts. For example, students may analyze air pollution data from their local community and propose strategies to reduce pollution levels. This approach encourages students to think critically about environmental issues and develop practical problem-solving abilities.

6. Hypothetical inquiry

Hypothetical inquiry engages students in using hypotheses to explain phenomena and make predictions. Students propose explanations based on their scientific knowledge and then test their hypotheses through experimentation or analysis. For instance, students may develop hypotheses about the impact of deforestation on local climate patterns and use climate data to evaluate their predictions.

By incorporating these approaches into Environmental Physics learning, students develop scientific inquiry skills, critical thinking abilities, and effective communication skills. They learn to observe, question, analyze data, propose explanations, and communicate their findings, fostering a deeper understanding of the subject matter and its relevance to real-world environmental challenges.

2. *Problem Based Learning (PBL)*

Problem-Based Learning (PBL) is an instructional approach that involves presenting students with real-world problems as a starting point for their learning. The problems are introduced to students before they have a complete understanding of the related concepts or materials, which stimulates their curiosity and drives their motivation to seek the necessary knowledge and skills to solve the problem.

PBL is characterized by the interaction between stimulus and response, where the learning environment provides students with both assistance and challenges in the form of problems. The brain's nervous system processes the stimuli effectively, allowing students to investigate, assess, analyze, and search for optimal solutions. This approach encourages active engagement and critical thinking skills in students.

Stage	Syntax
1	Student orientation to problems
2	Organizing students to learn
3	Guiding individual and group investigations .
4	Develop and present the work
5	Analyze and evaluate the situation solving process

Table 3
Syntax of Problem Based Learning (PBL)

PBL serves as a learning model that presents contextual problems to stimulate students' learning process. It challenges students to work collaboratively in groups to find solutions to real-world problems. The stages and syntax of PBL are outlined in Table 3, providing a framework for the implementation of this learning approach.

Here is a detailed explanation of each stage :

1. Student orientation to problems

In this stage, students are introduced to the problem or real-world situation that they will be working on. They become aware of the problem's context, relevance, and potential impact. For example, in an Environmental Physics class, students may be presented with a problem related to reducing energy consumption in their school to mitigate the environmental impact.

Example: Students are given the task of identifying energy-efficient alternatives for lighting systems in their school and analyzing the potential cost savings and environmental benefits.

2. Organizing students to learn

Students are organized into small groups to foster collaboration and teamwork. They begin to explore the problem collectively, share their initial thoughts and perspectives, and discuss possible approaches to finding a solution.

Example: Students form groups and brainstorm ideas for implementing energy-saving measures in their school. They discuss different lighting technologies, gather information on energy consumption, and propose strategies for reducing energy usage.

3. Guiding individual and group investigations

Students engage in individual and group investigations to gather relevant information and resources. They conduct research, analyze data, and apply their existing knowledge and skills to understand the problem better and develop potential solutions.

Example: Students research different lighting systems, compare their energy efficiency and environmental impact, and explore case studies of schools that have successfully implemented energy-saving measures. They also investigate local regulations and policies related to energy conservation.

4. Develop and present the work

Students develop their solutions or strategies to address the problem based on their investigations and analysis. They may create prototypes, conduct experiments, design plans, or propose policy changes. The final work or solution is presented to the class or a wider audience.

Example: Students design a comprehensive energy management plan for their school, including recommendations for replacing traditional lighting with energy-efficient alternatives, implementing motion sensor technology, and raising awareness among students and staff. They create visual presentations and deliver persuasive speeches to showcase their proposed solutions.

5. Analyze and evaluate the situation-solving process

Students reflect on their problem-solving process, evaluate the success of their tactics, analyze the effects of their solutions, and consider alternate ways at this stage. They evaluate their work's strengths and faults and identify opportunities for development.

Example: Students evaluate the energy-saving measures put in place at their school and collect statistics on energy use before and after the adjustments. They examine the cost-effectiveness of their ideas and remark on the problems encountered during deployment. They propose alternate ways that might improve energy efficiency even further.

Table 3 provides a structured overview of the stages involved in the PBL approach. It highlights the progression of activities, from problem orientation to solution development and evaluation. By engaging in PBL, students are motivated to explore and understand complex problems, collaborate with peers, develop critical thinking skills, and apply their knowledge to real-world contexts. The process of inquiry and problem-solving fosters deeper learning and enhances students' ability to transfer their knowledge and skills to new situations.

3. *Project-Based Learning (PjBL)*

Project-Based Learning (PjBL) is an instructional method that utilizes projects or activities as the primary medium of learning. This approach requires students to engage in exploration, assessment, interpretation, synthesis, and information gathering to produce various forms of learning outcomes. PjBL focuses on student-centered learning, allowing students to undertake in-depth investigations of specific topics.

In PjBL, students actively and constructively deepen their learning through a research-based approach. They tackle serious, accurate, and relevant problems or questions related to the project topic. This learning model encourages students to delve into the subject matter, apply critical thinking skills, and produce meaningful and tangible outcomes.

Stage	Syntax
1	Define basic questions .
2	Making project designs .
3	Scheduling
4	Monitor project progress
5	Result assessment
6	Experience evaluation

Table 4

Synthax of Project-Based Learning (PjBL)

The stages and syntax of PjBL are outlined in Table 4, providing a framework for implementing this approach. Here is a detailed explanation of each stage :

1. Define basic questions

Students begin by identifying and defining the fundamental questions that will guide their project. These questions serve as a foundation for their research and investigation. They should be open-ended and require critical thinking and problem-solving.

Example: In an environmental science project, students may define the question: "How can we reduce plastic waste in our school to promote environmental sustainability?"

2. Making project designs

In this stage, students develop a project design that outlines their plans and strategies for completing the project. They consider the resources, methods, and timeline required to achieve their goals. The design should be comprehensive and address all aspects of the project.

Example: Students create a project design that includes research on plastic waste management, collection and analysis of data on current waste practices in the school, the development of a waste reduction plan, and the implementation of initiatives such as recycling programs or awareness campaigns.

3. Scheduling

Students create a schedule or timeline to manage their project. They allocate time for various tasks, set milestones, and establish deadlines to ensure progress and timely completion. Scheduling helps students stay organized and on track throughout the project.

Example: Students create a timeline that includes specific deadlines for conducting research, collecting data, developing the waste reduction plan, implementing initiatives, and evaluating the outcomes. They set milestones to track their progress and ensure that each task is completed within the allocated time frame.

4. Monitor project progress

In this stage, students regularly monitor and track the progress of their project. They assess their progress against the project design and make adjustments as needed. They may seek guidance or support from the teacher or peers if they encounter challenges.

Example: Students hold regular check-in meetings to discuss their progress, share updates, and address any obstacles they face. They reflect on their achievements, identify areas where they may need additional support, and make necessary adjustments to ensure the project stays on track.

5. Result assessment

Students evaluate the outcomes and results of their project work. They assess the quality, accuracy, and relevance of their work based on predefined criteria or rubrics. This assessment helps students determine the effectiveness of their project and identify areas for improvement.

Example: Students evaluate the success of their waste reduction initiatives by measuring the amount of plastic waste reduced, conducting surveys to gauge changes in attitudes and behaviors, and assessing the overall impact on the school's environmental sustainability. They compare their outcomes against the goals outlined in their project design.

6. Experience evaluation

In this final stage, students reflect on their overall project experience. They evaluate the process, identify lessons learned, and consider ways to improve their approach for future projects. This stage promotes metacognition and self-reflection.

Example: Students reflect on their collaboration as a team, the effectiveness of their research methods, the challenges they faced, and the skills they developed throughout the project. They identify strengths and areas for improvement, and propose recommendations for future project implementations.

The objectives of Project-Based Learning include enhancing students' problem-solving abilities, acquiring new knowledge and skills, fostering active engagement in solving complex project problems with accurate outcomes, developing and improving students' skills in managing materials or tools for task completion, and promoting collaboration among students, particularly in group-based PjBL.

Table 4 provides a structured overview of the stages involved in the PjBL approach. It emphasizes the importance of defining questions, designing projects, scheduling tasks, monitoring progress, assessing results, and evaluating the overall experience. Through PjBL, students develop a deeper understanding of the subject matter, apply their learning to real-world contexts, collaborate with peers, and gain essential skills for project management and problem-solving. This approach encourages active engagement, critical thinking, creativity, and self-directed learning.

IV. CONCLUSION

The integration of Inquiry-Based Learning (IBL), Problem-Based Learning (PBL), and Project-Based Learning (PjBL) in Environmental Physics education has significant implications for student learning outcomes and experiences.

IBL, with its emphasis on student-driven inquiry and problem-solving, cultivates a sense of curiosity and empowers students to seek answers, develop theories, and explore the world around them. By implementing IBL principles, teachers assume the role of motivators who engage students in meaningful interactions and enhance their abilities. Students become active participants in their learning journey, formulating questions, conducting investigations, and analyzing data to construct their knowledge of environmental physics. The IBL approach encourages critical thinking, creativity, and independent inquiry, enabling students to develop a deeper understanding of the subject matter.

For instance, in an IBL activity, students might be presented with a real-world environmental issue, such as water pollution in a local river. They would explore the causes, consequences, and potential solutions to this problem. Through this process, they not only acquire knowledge of the underlying physics principles but also develop critical thinking skills as they evaluate evidence, propose explanations, and draw conclusions. IBL encourages students to take ownership of their learning, fostering a deep sense of engagement and motivation.

PBL, when applied to environmental issues, contributes to the development of students' ecological problem-solving skills. Beyond acquiring knowledge of physical science content in environmental physics, students are encouraged to find solutions to real environmental challenges they encounter. The PBL approach allows for diverse problem-solving approaches, enabling students to explore various alternatives and propose actionable solutions to improve the environment. By working collaboratively in groups, students engage in meaningful discussions, share ideas, and draw upon each other's strengths to address complex problems. The authentic context of PBL promotes the creation of practical and relevant solutions that address real-world environmental problems.

Students could be required to develop a sustainable energy system for their school or community as part of a PBL project, for instance. They would investigate various energy sources, evaluate their effects on the environment, and suggest an energy strategy that maximizes efficiency and reduces carbon emissions. Students learn to apply their understanding of physics concepts while also honing their critical thinking, collaboration, and communication abilities via this project. Students actively engage in problem-solving and develop creative solutions in PBL's active and dynamic learning environment.

PjBL, closely linked to inquiry-based activities, introduces problems or driving questions at the beginning of the learning process. Through PjBL, students engage in collaborative work and investigations guided by the facilitator (teacher). This approach promotes active learning and allows students to delve deeply into the subject matter, explore different perspectives, and develop comprehensive solutions to ecological physics problems. PjBL nurtures students' critical thinking, creativity, and practical skills in addressing environmental challenges.

Students may encounter a real-world issue in a PjBL project, such as how deforestation affects biodiversity in a nearby area. They would carry out study, gather information, and suggest mitigation plans for the environmental effects. Students actively cooperate, examine intricate data, and create solutions that take into consideration the multidisciplinary character of environmental physics throughout the project. Students have the chance to apply their knowledge and abilities in a meaningful and all-encompassing way through PjBL, which promotes a better comprehension of environmental challenges and its interconnection.

By integrating IBL, PBL, and PjBL in Environmental Physics education, student interest and engagement are heightened. Students learn through interactive and collaborative experiences, actively participating in problem-solving and generating real-world solutions and innovative ideas. This integrated approach nurtures students' critical thinking, creativity, and practical skills in addressing environmental challenges.

To summarize, the integration of IBL, PBL, and PjBL in Environmental Physics education creates a comprehensive and dynamic learning environment. It empowers students to inquire, problem-solve, and propose practical solutions to environmental issues. By integrating these three learning models, educators can enhance student interest, facilitate active engagement, and foster the development of critical skills needed to address complex ecological problems. The integration of IBL, PBL, and PjBL in Environmental Physics education paves the way for a transformative learning experience that equips students with the knowledge, skills, and mindset necessary to become active participants in addressing environmental challenges and shaping a sustainable future.

REFERENCES

Bosch, E., Seifried, E., & Spinath, B. (2021). What successful students do: Evidence-based learning activities matter for students' performance in higher education beyond prior knowledge, motivation, and prior achievement. Learning and Individual Differences, 91, 102056.

Cheung, H. Y., & Chan, A. W. H. (2011). The relationship of competitiveness motive on people's happiness through education. International Journal of Intercultural Relations, 35, 179–185.

Decker-Lange, C. (2018). Problem- and inquiry-based learning in alternative contexts: Using museums in management education. The International Journal of Management Education, 16, 446–459.

Elfelly, N., Dieulot, J. Y., Benrejeb, M., & Borne, P. (2010). A new multimodel approach for complex processes modeling based on classification algorithms: Experimental validation. IFAC Proceedings, 43, 480–486.

Furtak, E. M., Bakeman, R., & Buell, J. Y. (2018). Developing knowledge-in-action with a learning progression: Sequential analysis of teachers' questions and responses to student ideas. Teaching and Teacher Education, 76, 267–282.

Gómez-Tejedor, J. A., Vidaurre, A., Tort-Ausina, I., Molina-Mateo, J., Serrano, M. A., Meseguer-Dueñas, J. M., Martínez Sala, R. M., Quiles, S., & Riera, J. (2020). Effectiveness of flip teaching on engineering students' performance in the physics lab. Computers & Education, 144, 103708.

Guo, P., Saab, N., Post, L. S., & Admiraal, W. (2020). A review of project-based learning in higher education: Student outcomes and measures. International Journal of Educational Research, 102, 101586.

Kreutzmann, J. C., Marin, M. F., Fendt, M., Milad, M. R., Ressler, K., & Jovanovic, T. (2021). Unconditioned response to an aversive stimulus as predictor of response to conditioned fear and safety: A cross-species study. Behavioural Brain Research, 402, 113105.

Lamnina, M., & Chase, C. C. (2019). Developing a thirst for knowledge: How uncertainty in the classroom influences curiosity, affect, learning, and transfer. Contemporary Educational Psychology, 59, 101785.

Lerum, Ø., Eikeland Tjomsland, H., Leirhaug, P. E., McKenna, J., Quaramby, T., Bartholomew, J., Jenssen, E. S., Smith, A.-D., & Resaland, G. K. (2021). The Conforming, The Innovating and The Connecting Teacher: A qualitative study of why teachers in lower secondary school adopt physically active learning. Teaching and Teacher Education, 105, 103434.

Lin, H.-H., Yen, W.-C., & Wang, Y.-S. (2018). Investigating the effect of learning method and motivation on learning performance in a business simulation system context: An experimental study. Computers & Education, 127, 30–40.

Martin, A. J., & Evans, P. (2018). Load reduction instruction: Exploring a framework that assesses explicit instruction through independent learning. Teaching and Teacher Education, 73, 203–214.

Matewos, A. M., Marsh, J. A., McKibben, S., Sinatra, G. M., Le, Q. T., & Polikoff, M. S. (2019). Teacher learning from supplementary curricular materials: Shifting instructional roles. Teaching and Teacher Education, 83, 212–224.

Murphy, B., Mallett, L., & Law, M. (2017). Family Education Program Improves Diet, Family Meals, and Physical Activity with Interactive Demonstrations. Journal of Nutrition Education and Behavior, 49, 36–37.

Napitupulu, N. D. (2022). The urgency of the multi-model approach in learning environmental physics to achieve learning goals. World Journal of Advanced Research and Reviews, 13(3), 431–437.

Newton, X. A., & Tonelli, E. P. (2020). Building undergraduate STEM majors' capacity for delivering inquiry-based mathematics and science lessons: An exploratory evaluation study. Studies in Educational Evaluation, 64, 100833.

Pan, G., Shankararaman, V., Koh, K., & Gan, S. (2021). Students' evaluation of teaching in the project-based learning programme: An instrument and a development process. The International Journal of Management Education, 19, 100501.

Parfilova, G. G., & Kalimullin, A. M. (2014). Research of Russian Students' Ecological Competency. Procedia - Social and Behavioral Sciences, 131, 35–39.

Peterson, E. G. (2020). Supporting curiosity in schools and classrooms. Current Opinion in Behavioral Sciences, 35, 7–13.

Renuka, G. (2021). Innovative teaching and learning strategies for materials engineering education. Materials Today: Proceedings, S2214785321032703.

Rovers, S. F. E., Clarebout, G., Savelberg, H. H. C. M., & van Merriënboer, J. J. G. (2018). Improving student expectations of learning in a problem-based environment. Computers in Human Behavior, 87, 416–423.

Schulz, R., & Mandzuk, D. (2005). Learning to teach, learning to inquire: A 3-year study of teacher candidates' experiences. Teaching and Teacher Education, 21, 315–331.

Schnell, C., & Loerwald, D. (2019). Interest as an influencing factor on student achievement in Economics. International Review of Economics Education, 30, 100130.

Shawer, S. F. (2017). Teacher-driven curriculum development at the classroom level: Implications for curriculum, pedagogy and teacher training. Teaching and Teacher Education, 63, 296–313.

Souza, A. D., & Vaswani, V. (2020). Diversity in approach to teaching and assessing ethics education for medical undergraduates: A scoping review. Annals of Medicine and Surgery, 56, 178–185.

Svirko, E., Gabbott, E., Badger, J., & Mellanby, J. (2019). Does acquisition of hypothetical conditional sentences contribute to understanding the principles of scientific enquiry? Cognitive Development, 51, 46–57.

Stratton, D. H. (2020). Types of instructional strategies and their effect on Preparation for Future Learning in differentiation. International Journal of Educational Research, 104, 101691.

Voet, M., & De Wever, B. (2017). Preparing pre-service history teachers for organizing inquiry-based learning: The effects of an introductory training program. Teaching and Teacher Education, 63, 206–217.

Wahlsten, D. (2019). The Nervous System Genes, Brain Function, and Behavior (Elsevier), 31–50.

Wang, J., Guo, D., & Jou, M. (2015). A study on the effects of model-based inquiry pedagogy on students' inquiry skills in a virtual physics lab. Computers in Human Behavior, 49, 658–669.

Wang, P. H., Wu, P. L., Yu, K. W., & Lin, Y. X. (2015). Influence of Implementing Inquiry-based Instruction on Science Learning Motivation and Interest: A Perspective of Comparison. Procedia - Social and Behavioral Sciences, 174, 1292–1299.

Williams, C. C., Hecker, K. G., Paget, M. K., Coderre, S. P., Burak, K. W., Wright, B., & Krigolson, O. E. (2018). The application of reward learning in the real world: Changes in the reward positivity amplitude reflect learning in a medical education context. International Journal of Psychophysiology, 132, 236–242.

Wood, R., & Shirazi, S. (2020). A systematic review of audience response systems for teaching and learning in higher education: The student experience. Computers & Education, 153, 103896.

Zouganeli, E., Tyssø, V., Feng, B., Arnesen, K., & Kapetanovic, N. (2014). Project-based learning in programming classes – the effect of open project scope on student motivation and learning outcome. IFAC Proceedings, 47, 12232–12236.

About The Author

Nurasyah Dewi Napitupulu is an esteemed educator and researcher in the field of Physics Education. She holds a position as a faculty member at the Department of Physics Education, Faculty of Teacher Training and Education at Tadulako University in Indonesia. With a passion for innovative teaching and learning approaches, Nurasyah has dedicated her career to improving the quality of education in the field of Environmental Physics.

Nurasyah has a strong academic background, having obtained her Bachelor's degree in Physics Education and a Master's degree in Education. Her expertise lies in the integration of different learning models to enhance student engagement, critical thinking, and problem-solving skills in the context of Environmental Physics. She believes in the importance of providing students with a holistic learning experience that prepares them for real-world challenges.

Throughout her career, Nurasyah has actively participated in research projects focused on the application of multi-model approaches in Physics Education. Her research interests also include inquiry-based learning, problem-based learning, and project-based learning. She has published several articles in reputable journals, contributing to the advancement of knowledge and practice in the field.

In addition to her research contributions, Nurasyah is a dedicated educator who strives to create an inclusive and interactive learning environment for her students. She actively engages in curriculum development and instructional design to ensure that students receive a comprehensive and meaningful learning experience. Her teaching methods emphasize active learning, critical thinking, and the integration of technology to enhance student engagement and understanding.

Nurasyah is committed to sharing her expertise and experiences with fellow educators, participating in conferences, workshops, and seminars. She believes in the power of collaboration and continues to collaborate with colleagues and researchers both nationally and internationally to advance the field of Physics Education.

"The Urgency of the Multi-Model Approach in Learning Environmental Physics to Achieve Learning Goals" is a culmination of Nurasyah's extensive research and experience in the field. Through this book, she aims to provide educators with valuable insights and practical strategies for incorporating multi-model approaches into Environmental Physics education. Nurasyah's dedication to improving teaching and learning practices makes her a respected figure in the field of Physics Education.

www.ingramcontent.com/pod-product-compliance
Lightning Source LLC
Chambersburg PA
CBHW071612270726
48661CB00019B/2611